MAISON MARGIELA

ARTISANAL 2024

WOULD YOU LIKE TO TAKE A WALK WITH ME... OFFLINE?

JOHN GALLIANO

PHOTOGRAPHS BY

PAOLO ROVERSI

STYLING BY

JOHN GALLIANO

ALEXIS ROCHE

MAKE-UP BY

DAME PAT McGRATH

HAIR BY

EUGENE SOULEIMAN

PUBLISHED BY

LUNCHEON EDITIONS

For this special *Luncheon* edition, on 25th and 26th June 2024 a team numbering close to a hundred came together at the Maison Margiela HQ in the 16th arrondissement of Paris to create these beautiful photographs taken by Paolo Roversi of the Artisanal 2024 collection by John Galliano. A few months later in September John and Paolo sat down in Paolo's studio in the 14th arrondissement to discuss their work together over the years since first meeting in 1985, John's inspirations behind this collection and the photographic techniques used in the making of these pictures. Featured alongside the series of photographs of 'Looks' is a glossary of the unique vocabulary used by Maison Margiela.

LOOKS

PAGE 4

ARTISANALOGY

PAGE 38

PORTRAIT OF THE ARTIST

PAGE 50

CONVERSATION

PAGE 51

PORTRAIT OF THE MUSE

PAGE 55

INSPIRATIONS

PAGE 56

CREDITS

PAGE 78

LOOK 21B

SANIJA wears off-white foam 'reverse swatching' jacket and skirt enveloped in cellophane worn over an ecru calico corset underpinned by a silicone prothèse matching the skin tone of the muse. Worn with papier-mâché, clay, string and stretch-tulle lay doll gloves overlaid with white silk jersey, silk stockings matching the skin tone of the muse and white leather pumps by Christian Louboutin for Maison Margiela.

Please see ARTISANALOGY on page 38 for a glossary of 'Look' vocabulary.

LOOK 27

CHOL wears carton-coloured cotton 'caisetted' cape cut with 'the memory of' an ulster coat, worn over a patinaed knitted silk bodysuit underpinned by a corset covered in jersey and a silicone hip prothèse matching the skin tone of the muse. A taped 'reverse swatching' hat in white foam and 'caisetted' cotton, a small top-handle 'Snatched' bag enveloped in tape and 'caisetted' cotton, patinaed knitted silk stockings matching the skin tone of the muse, papier-mâché, clay, string and stretch-tulle lay doll gloves overlaid in beige jersey. Rust-coloured velour and faux lizard Tabi ankle-strap two-piece heels by Christian Louboutin for Maison Margiela.

LOOK 21

NATASHA wears a white foam 'reverse swatching' jacket enveloped in black stocking material worn over a 'reverse swatching' bustier dress composed of a 'bianchetto' cotton toile bustier and a white foam skirt enveloped in black stocking material, and a stretch-tulle illusion 'reverse swatching' Cadolle high-neck body matching the skin tone of the muse, enveloped in black stocking material. A white leather 'reverse swatching' 'Snatched' bag enveloped in black and beige stocking material, a white foam 'reverse swatching' hat enveloped in black stocking material. Papier-mâché, clay, string and stretch-tulle lay doll gloves overlaid in beige jersey. White platform pumps created by Christian Louboutin for Natasha Poonawalla.

LOOK 43

NYAKIER wears blue-and-white striped cotton poplin 'stripe-tease' blouse worn under a blue-and-white striped cotton poplin 'stripe-tease' corset with a white cotton organdie full skirt overlaid with cellophane, a silk knitted bodysuit and a silicone hip prothèse matching the skin tone of the muse. A wood-imitation moulded leather breastplate, a white leather small top-handle 'Snatched' bag, silk stockings, and merkin. Papier-mâché, clay, string and stretch-tulle lay doll gloves overlaid in silk jersey matching the skin tone of the muse and black leather Tabi pumps by Christian Louboutin for Maison Margiela.

LOOK 41

REJOICE wears blue-and-white striped cotton poplin 'stripe-tease' sundress worn over a silk knitted bodysuit, a jersey covered corset and a silicone hip prothèse all matching the skin tone of the muse. A wood-imitation moulded leather breastplate, a white leather small top-handled 'Snatched' bag, papier-mâché, clay, string and stretch-tulle lay doll gloves overlaid in silk jersey matching the skin tone of the muse and black leather Tabi pumps by Christian Louboutin for Maison Margiela.

LOOK 16

MAMUOR wears ulster coat in a 'milletrage' composed of black satin lining, white triple organza, white felt, anthracite chevron-printed wool crêpe and an 'aquarelled' tulle voilette with a moon-faded print, worn with a black wool polo neck, 'the memory of' a trouser in a 'milletrage' composed of black silk lining, white double organza, white felt and brown tweed texture-printed wool crêpe worn over black silk organza pyjama trousers cut into shorts underpinned by a cognac-coloured leather cincher. A windowpane-printed 'emotional-cut' wool crêpe cap, black and green jacquard socks, and black croc-embossed leather Tabi lace-up brogue boots by Christian Louboutin for Maison Margiela.

PREVIOUS PAGES

LOOK 38B

CANLAN wears white cotton tarlatan jacket worn over an ecru calico corset underpinned by a silicone hip prothèse matching the skin tone of the muse. A merkin in synthetic hair and tulle illusion matching the skin tone of the muse and a beige silk taffeta pencil skirt with 'retrograding' in silicone and 'retrograded' seams. Worn with red leather gloves and pony skin Tabi knee-high boots with hand-painted 'retrograding' by Christian Louboutin for Maison Margiela.

LOOK 36B

SHERRY wears white cotton tarlatan coat worn over an ecru calico corset underpinned by a silicone hip prothèse matching the skin tone of the muse. Worn with pale green taffeta gloves 'retrograded' with silicone and pony skin Tabi knee-high boots with hand-painted 'retrograding' by Christian Louboutin for Maison Margiela.

LOOK 40B

HAMIN wears ecru calico trouser suit toile worn over an ecru calico corset. Worn with beige taffeta gloves 'retrograded' with silicone, black silk socks, and black Tabi lace-up derbies by Christian Louboutin and pony skin spats with hand-painted 'retrograding' by Christian Louboutin for Maison Margiela.

FOLLOWING PAGES

LOOK 29

VALENTINE wears black silk tulle 'seamlace' dress worn over a patinaed knitted cotton bodysuit matching the skin tone of the muse. A boudoir-coloured silk satin cincher underpinned by a silicone hip prothèse matching the skin tone of the muse. An ecru foam 'reverse swatchting' bra enveloped in black and beige stocking material. A merkin in synthetic hair and tulle illusion matching the skin tone of the muse. A wood-imitation moulded leather breastplate, patinaed knitted silk stockings matching the skin tone of the muse and papier-mâché, clay, string and stretch tulle lay doll gloves overlaid in beige silk jersey. Worn with black leather Tabi pumps by Christian Louboutin for Maison Margiela.

LOOK 28

LEA wears boudoir-coloured tulle dress with 'retrograding' in rosette-band appliqué bands re-embroidered with iridescent crystals and star motifs cut from mirror fragments. Worn over a charcoal-coloured knitted silk bodysuit, a boudoir-coloured silk satin cincher underpinned by a silicone hip prothèse matching the skin tone of the muse. A merkin in synthetic hair and tulle illusion. A charcoal foam 'reverse swatching' bra enveloped in black, charcoal and beige stocking material. A wood-imitation moulded leather breastplate, a white foam 'reverse swatching' hat enveloped in black and grey stocking material, patinaed charcoal knitted silk stockings and papier-mâché, clay, string and stretch-tulle lay doll gloves overlaid in charcoal silk jersey. Worn with black leather Tabi pumps by Christian Louboutin for Maison Margiela.

LOOK 24

THOMAS wears brown tweed 'rétrécirage' jacket worn over a patinaed knitted silk and velvet body matching the skin tone of the muse, trousers with vermillion lampasses in a 'milletrage' composed of black silk lining, white double organza, white felt and check-printed wool crêpe, and a black leather cincher. A white cotton detachable collar, a bow tie repurposed from antique silk twill, a wood-imitation moulded leather breastplate, and a black felt bowler hat enveloped in beige stocking material, and papier-mâché, clay, string and stretch-tulle lay doll gloves overlaid in beige jersey. Black leather Tabi lace-up boots enveloped in beige stocking material by Christian Louboutin for Maison Margiela.

LOOK 45

MONICA wears black silk chiffon short sleeved 'abstract lace' draped bias-cut blouse worn with a beige silk taffeta pencil skirt with 'retrograding' in silicone and 'retrograded' seams. Black silk chiffon 'abstract lace' bloomers, a boudoir-coloured silk satin cincher underpinned by a silicone hip prothèse matching the skin tone of the muse. A patinaed knitted cotton bodysuit matching the skin tone of the muse, a merkin in synthetic hair and tulle illusion, beige knitted silk stockings, papier-mâché, clay, string and stretch tulle lay doll gloves overlaid in beige silk jersey, and a porcelain-imitation moulded leather breastplate. Worn with black patent studded platform slingback pumps by Maison Margiela.

LOOK 4

TISH wears black silk 'aquarelled' tulle dress worn over a boudoir-coloured tulle illusion skirt with 'retrograding' in black handkerchief appliqué, underpinned by a boudoir-coloured silk satin cincher and a silicone hip prothèse matching the skin tone of the muse. A merkin in synthetic hair and tulle illusion matching the skin tone of the muse, and black Tabi neoprene interlaced ankle-strap pumps by Christian Louboutin for Maison Margiela.

LOOK 3

TESS wears black 'aquarelled' tulle illusion dress with 'retrograding' in black silk mousseline handkerchief-scalloped appliqué, worn over a boudoir-coloured silk satin cincher underpinned by a silicone hip prothèse matching the skin tone of the muse. A merkin in synthetic hair and tulle illusion matching the skin tone of the muse, and black neoprene Tabi interlaced ankle-strap pumps by Christian Louboutin for Maison Margiela.

LOOK 33

JUM wears grey chalk-stripe flannel trouser-suit imbued with the 'emotional cut' of a shield gesture and 'gouttoir-coated' with seeping silicone and hand-embroidered crystal raindrop beading, with a 'gouttoir-coated' hem, worn over a black silk satin cincher and bordeaux felt suspenders. A black washed barathea 'emotional-cut' cap 'gouttoir-coated' with seeping silicone and hand-embroidered crystal raindrop beading, a deconstructed snakeskin-handle black nylon umbrella 'gouttoir-coated' with seeping silicone, and black leather Tabi lace-up derbies by Christian Louboutin for Maison Margiela.

LOOK 44

GWENDOLINE wears overdress and an underdress in white silk taffeta with 'retrograding' in seeping silicone coating worn over a blue-and-white striped cotton poplin 'stripe-tease' corset and a white silk knitted bodysuit, underpinned by a silicone hip prothèse matching the skin tone of the muse. A porcelain-imitation moulded leather breastplate, a white leather small top-handle 'Snatched' bag, white silk stockings, and white papier-mâché, clay, string and stretch-tulle lay doll gloves overlaid in white silk jersey. White leather pumps by Christian Louboutin for Maison Margiela.

LOOK 17B

MAGGIE wears a pale beige boiled cashmere cardigan worn with an ivory-coloured crêpe-backed satin 'deshabillé' dress toile, cut with 'fabric sequins'. Worn over an ecru calico corset toile underpinned by a silicone hip prothèse matching the skin tone of the muse. Worn with papier-mâché, clay, string and stretch-tulle lay doll gloves overlaid with white silk jersey, an off-white foam 'reverse swatching' hat and white leather pumps by Christian Louboutin for Maison Margiela.

LOOK 26

DAIMY wears grey mélange tweed inside-out 'rétrécirage' jacket worn with a carton-coloured silk organza and crin 'caisetted' paper-doll skirt cut with the memory of a bow and a rickrack motif, over a patinaed knitted silk bodysuit matching the skin tone of the muse, underpinned by a boudoir-coloured silk satin cincher and a silicone hip prothèse matching the skin tone of the muse. A porcelain-imitation moulded leather breastplate, a 'reverse swatching' hat in white foam and orange and beige stocking material, a grey mélange tweed 'rétrécirage' small top-handle 'Snatched' bag enveloped in beige, orange and black fishnet stocking material, patinaed knitted silk stockings matching the skin tone of the muse, and papier-mâché, clay, string and stretch-tulle lay doll gloves overlaid in beige jersey. Beige leather Tabi pumps enveloped in beige, black and orange stocking material by Christian Louboutin for Maison Margiela.

LOOK 8

EMELINE wears black gloved Chantilly lace 'seamlace' dress encrusted with a papillon de nuit motif in silk velvet, silk satin, silk mousseline, silk georgette and silk tulle, underpinned by a boudoir-coloured silk satin cincher and a silicone hip prothèse matching the skin tone of the muse. A merkin in synthetic hair and tulle illusion matching the skin tone of the muse, and black neoprene Tabi interlaced ankle-strap pumps by Christian Louboutin for Maison Margiela.

OPPOSITE AND FOLLOWING PAGES

LOOK 1

LEON wears an ecru calico corset. Worn with an 'emotional-cut' printed wool crêpe cap, black silk socks and black leather lace-up Tabi derbies by Christian Louboutin for Maison Margiela.

LOOK 35

YERAY wears an ecru calico corset toile. Worn with an 'emotional-cut' printed wool crêpe cap, black silk socks and black leather lace-up Tabi derbies by Christian Louboutin for Maison Margiela.

ARTISANALOGY

THE 5AC

ORIGIN: DÉFILÉ COLLECTION SPRING-SUMMER 2016

The 5AC is the signature handbag of Maison Margiela continuously interpreted by the house in a variety of styles. A subverted modern classic, the bag employs the technique of *anonymity of the lining* to reveal its internal structure: an extension of the lining, which transforms the bag's shape to expose a larger pocket adorned with the four stitches. Its name is derived from '133t speak', an early tech language that encodes the word 'SAC' – French for bag – into '5AC'.

ABSTRACT LACE

ORIGIN: ARTISANAL COLLECTION AUTUMN-WINTER 2019

Abstract lace refers to technique of evenly riddling a garment with holes – either cut by hand or machine – as a deconstructive interpretation of polka dots, effectively creating an abstraction of lace.

ANONYMITY OF THE LINING

ORIGIN: ARTISANAL COLLECTION SPRING-SUMMER 2016

Anonymity of the lining is a technique defined by the revelation of a garment's interior construction. Through cutting, elements such as lining, threading, facing, and interfacing – the authentic core of dress-making – surface from within and become decoration in their own right.

APPROPRIATING THE INAPPROPRIATE

ORIGIN: ARTISANAL COLLECTION SPRING-SUMMER 2018

Appropriating the inappropriate describes a code-switch between two classic wardrobe staples foreign to each other by nature. It can be the adaptation of haute couture fabrics into sportswear, the employment of technical materials in high dressmaking, or the infiltration of motifs native to one genre of dress into another. It is the texture of knitwear forged in rubber, a riding jacket mutated with a bustier, or a hooded bathrobe transformed into an evening dress.

AQUARELLING

ORIGIN: ARTISANAL COLLECTION 2024

Aquarelling is a term used for the draping of tulle or muslin in the same way a painter works with watercolours. Often applied in tandem with strategically-printed transparent fabrics, it can also be employed to create the illusion of gestures, imprints or anatomical shapes within garments. The technique is loosely related to *wet look* and *circular cutting*.

ARTISANAL

ORIGIN: WOMEN'S COLLECTION SPRING-SUMMER 1989

Artisanal is the term used by Maison Margiela for its haute couture collections for which the house gained the official appellation by the Chambre Syndicale de la Haute Couture in 2012. Under the creative direction of John Galliano, the ideas, techniques and proposals developed for the Artisanal collection inform every other aspect of the house, through the *prêt-à-porter* and *avant-première* lines. The term *Artisanal* – meaning 'non-mechanised' – was originally used by Martin Margiela since 1989 for designs repurposed from existing garments, a premise which also underpinned the founder's first Artisanal collection in 2006.

BIANCHETTO

ORIGIN: WOMEN'S COLLECTION SPRING-SUMMER 1989

Bianchetto is the white overpaint technique exercised by Maison Margiela as a distinguishing signature. The effect, which conveys *the memory of* the strokes of the paintbrush, is employed on garments, accessories, objects or interiors as a means of reducing the surface of an entity to a white canvas. Here, traces of time and use become visible, expressing the soul of history and human contact. *Bianchetto* was introduced in 1989 by Martin Margiela, who first overpainted a collection of Salvation Army furniture for the Maison's studio.

BIAS CUTTING

ORIGIN: ARTISANAL MEN'S COLLECTION AUTUMN-WINTER 2018

Bias cutting materialises when a fabric is cut at an angle, allowing the natural elasticity of the cloth to hit the bias. Contrary to cutting straight-of-grain, the technique creates a languid and mercurial garment, which generates a harmonious and dynamic exchange between fabric and body. The result is a liberating and non-constricting sense of movement. *Bias cutting* is the dressmaking practice through which John Galliano has historically expressed himself.

BIRD-PECKING

ORIGIN: ARTISANAL COLLECTION 2021

Bird-pecking is a technique wherein a fabric is evenly cut into – either by hand or by laser – to form flickering turret-like holes evocative of those hacked out of bark by a beak, revealing the lining of a garment.

THE BLOUSE BLANCHE

ORIGIN: WOMEN'S COLLECTION SPRING-SUMMER 1989

The blouse blanche is the white cotton coat historically worn by those who work within Maison Margiela. In 1989, before the house was granted its own haute couture appellation in 2012, it was introduced by Martin Margiela as a token of respect for the haute couture houses of Paris, whose *petites-mains* traditionally wear white coats. Today, the *blouse blanche* serves as an ode to the Maison's Artisanal haute couture ateliers. An identifying feature of the brand, it often translates into its collections.

THE BOURGEOIS GESTURE

ORIGIN: ARTISANAL COLLECTION SPRING-SUMMER 2020

The bourgeois gesture is a way of capturing in cutting or styling the blasé movements and signals popularly associated with a mid-century bourgeois fashion mentality and approach to the art of dressing. Here, societal uniforms are anthropomorphised through body language: the nonchalant shrug of a coat off the shoulder, the insolent tie of a bow, or the conscious drape of a plaid over the arm.

CAISETTING

ORIGIN: ARTISANAL COLLECTION AUTUMN-WINTER 2017

Caisetting is a technique in which fine materials like silk organza and crin are ridged and grooved to resemble corrugated cardboard. The practice is founded in the notion of *new glamour*, the elevation of simple or habitual materials through the familiar language of glamour. The *caisetted* texture can be hand-cut with motifs to evoke *the memory of* certain imagery or other garments. (While *caisetting* first appeared in the Autumn-Winter 2017 Artisanal collection, the technique was formally coined for the 2024 Artisanal collection.)

CENTRE CUTTING

ORIGIN: ARTISANAL COLLECTION 2022

Centre cutting creates a horizontal incision across a tailored garment through which one half of its volume is resized. The practice is typically employed in jackets and suits to create the memory of a smaller volume within the frame of the garment.

CIRCULAR CUTTING

ORIGIN: ARTISANAL COLLECTION AUTUMN-WINTER 2020

Circular cutting is a way of constructing garments in which the interaction of several circular panels sewn together disrupts the draping of the garment, creating a sculptural effect. John Galliano first explored the technique in 1987.

CO-ED

ORIGIN: CO-ED COLLECTION SPRING-SUMMER 2019

Co-Ed is an expression used by Maison Margiela to signify its *genderless* approach to design and dressing. It is derived from 'co-educational': the belief in not separating students of opposite sexes during their schooling.

DECADENT CUTTING

ORIGIN: ARTISANAL COLLECTION SPRING-SUMMER 2019

Decadent cutting characterises various ideas of reducing – or degenerating – garments or accessories to their most restrained construction, evoking the process of decadence itself. Drawing on the notion of *inverted excess*, the techniques are expressed in a purified approach to dressmaking: a flat-cut jacket, an all-in-one *combinaison*, or garments whose details fade away until only *the memory of* the garment itself is left.

DÉCORTIQUÉ

ORIGIN: ARTISANAL COLLECTION SPRING-SUMMER 2017

Décortiqué is the reduction of a garment or accessory to its core structure. Meaning to 'strip something of its outer layers', the technique exposes the essential frames of an item normally hidden from view by cutting out any areas and layers but the seams, boning or closures, which hold it together.

DRESSING IN HASTE

ORIGIN: ARTISANAL COLLECTION AUTUMN-WINTER 2017

Dressing in haste is a technique through which familiar spontaneous gestures and ritual actions of the routine dressing process are *freeze-framed* in the cuts and styling of garments and accessories. It is the *unconscious glamour* of slipping into a T-shirt, pulling on a coat, or wrapping a towel around one's head.

ELBOW KNITTING

ORIGIN: ARTISANAL COLLECTION 2022

Elbow knitting is a magnified form of knitting in which extra-large loops are used to structure highly voluminous garments.

EMOTIONAL CUTTING

ORIGIN: CO-ED COLLECTION SPRING-SUMMER 2024

Emotional cutting imbues a garment with the unconscious gestures with which we naturally imprint the clothes we wear: the shrug of a jacket, the cowing of a pocket, the runkling of a hem, a caban pulled over the head in the rain, a lapel raised to cover the face, or a trouser hoicked up to evade a water puddle. Established *emotional cuts* include the clutch gesture, the incognito gesture, the hoicked-up gesture, the shield gesture, the shelter gesture, and the *petit devant*. Evoked through techniques such as *circular cutting*, *emotional cutting* is founded in the gestural technical language continuously evolved by John Galliano at Maison Margiela including *dressing in haste*, *the bourgeois gesture*, and *unconscious glamour*.

ESSORAGE

ORIGIN: ARTISANAL COLLECTION 2021

Essorage is a technique wherein familiar garments – often made from vintage or overstock fabrics – are scaled up eight times their original dimension, only to be wrung into new shapes through size-compressing enzyme and stonewash treatments. In the process, fabrics erode and reveal their true colours, imbuing the garment with a trace of time and a sense of soul.

EXFOLIAGE

ORIGIN: CO-ED COLLECTION SPRING-SUMMER 2024

Exfoliage is a customisation-inspired technique through which the top layer of a garment such as a bustier is ripped away to reveal its inside construction, then lowered over a skirt and laminated with relief effect, essentially 'exfoliating' one garment to create a type of 'foliage' within another.

FABRIC PLUMAGE

ORIGIN: ARTISANAL COLLECTION 2022

Fabric plumage denotes the hacking up of the material of a garment to create the illusion of plume.

FABRIC SEQUINS

ORIGIN: ARTISANAL COLLECTION SPRING-SUMMER 2020

Fabric sequins signify the all-over scalloping of a garment – either cut by hand or machine – creating flickering holes that interact with the lining of the garment.

FILIGRADING

ORIGIN: THE MET GALA MAY 2024

A portmanteau of filigree and *retrograding*, *filigrading* evolves through hand-wired metalwork the practice of *retrograding* which denotes a dégradé of thread-work, appliqué or encrustation. The hand-embroidered technique incorporates silver metal formations of lace, flowers, leaves and sprigs interlinked with silver chain and floral motifs cut from mirror fragments, bedecked with crystal pendants, pearls and clasped bijoux, refracting the light in the manner of jewellery. The technique was introduced in the Artisanal look created for Kim Kardashian for the 2024 Met Gala.

FILTRAGE

ORIGIN: ARTISANAL COLLECTION SPRING-SUMMER 2017

Filtrage characterises the layering of one more translucent material over another material. Often employed in the creation of illusions, the interaction of these filters – their individual colours, adornments or effects – can be employed to form new impressions.

THE FOUR STITCHES

ORIGIN: WOMEN'S COLLECTION SPRING-SUMMER 1989

The four stitches are an identifying feature of Maison Margiela. The white slanted stitches appear on the exteriors of garments and accessories, while holding in place the interior fabric label with the house's signature numeric coding or blank logo. Forming *the memory of* a rectangle indicative of that label, *the four stitches* create a blank logo key to the Maison's code of anonymity.

FREEZE-FRAMING

ORIGIN: CO-ED COLLECTION 2023

Freeze-framing is a gestural form of cutting which captures *the memory of* the movement of a photographed garment and translates it into the contours of a new garment. It was first employed to render in tulle the movement of sculptural party dresses depicted in mid-century photography. Elements of *freeze-framing* appear in a number of Artisanal techniques such as *work-in-progress*.

GENDERLESS

ORIGIN: CO-ED COLLECTION SPRING-SUMMER 2019

Genderless is a term employed by Maison Margiela to describe its approach to design and dressing. Detecting a new reality, in September 2019 John Galliano merged his women's and men's *prêt-a-porter* shows into one *genderless* presentation known as *Co-Ed*. Henceforth, proposals created for the Maison's collections have been *genderless*. In its expansion of *genderless* codes, the Maison continuously studies the nature of traditionally *genderless* wardrobe staples such as the overcoat, the cape, or the *combinaison*.

THE GLAM SLAM

ORIGIN: DÉFILÉ COLLECTION SPRING-SUMMER 2018

The Glam Slam is the genderless signature bag of Maison Margiela continuously interpreted by the house in a variety of styles. With its rounded curves and soft cloud-like shape, the quilted bag evokes universal associations of comfort, reflecting the notions of *unconscious glamour* and *dressing in haste* key to the Maison. Inspired by images of travellers in transit, its design is founded in travelling rituals shared across cultures.

GOUTTOIR-COATING

ORIGIN: ARTISANAL COLLECTION 2024

Gouttoir-coating is a technique applied to articles of clothing whereby seeping silicone treatments as well as hand-beaded crystals are made to look as if they have been rained on or as if trouser hems have been dragged through puddles of rainwater.

HACKING

ORIGIN: ARTISANAL COLLECTION AUTUMN-WINTER 2018

Hacking describes the act of intercepting a garment or motif with the intention of transforming it into another type of garment or motif, or revealing its authentic properties. It can be an overcoat hacked up into a jacket, or the interruption of a fabric's *trompe l'oeil* print evoked like the accidental slip of a print machine, effectively exposing its illusion. The idea also appears in the *trompe l'oeil* tear effect used on the packaging of the Mutiny by Maison Margiela *eau de parfum*.

HEROIC CUTTING

ORIGIN: ARTISANAL COLLECTION AUTUMN-WINTER 2020

Heroic cutting is a form of deconstruction in which a chivalrous silhouette is conjured within a traditional garment by slashing its structure and re-composing it to evoke the shape of armour.

ICONS

ORIGIN: ICONS COLLECTION 2021

Icons are seasonless garments and accessories founded in enduring codes developed for Maison Margiela by Creative Director John Galliano. Identified by their red thread branding, the creations make up the *Icons* collection: the distilled *parfum* of the house. Permanently available in Maison Margiela stores, this line of key wardrobe pieces is seasonally re-evaluated and refined.

INVERTED SNOBBERY

ORIGIN: ARTISANAL COLLECTION 2021

Inverted snobbery is the idea of transposing the placement of fine and humble materials, giving new value to the latter. It is a re-contextualisation demonstrated in *pauvre* materials turned into desirable manifestations; or, the switching of adornments and underpinnings, like a humble toile coat lined in elaborate white-washed embroideries, or a faded coat lined in tea towelling fabric overlaid with laced devoré.

THE MEMORY OF

ORIGIN: ARTISANAL COLLECTION AUTUMN-WINTER 2017

The memory of illustrates the languished impression of a familiar motif still evident – either visibly or emotionally – within a garment, an accessory, or a piece of jewellery. It is the remaining outline of a classic wardrobe element known to all; an echo of something that once was, evoked within the creation of something new: *the memory of* a collar stitched onto a shirt, *the memory of* a crease flocked across the surface of a coat, or *the memory of* a swimsuit cut into a tailored jacket.

MILLEFEUILLE

ORIGIN: ARTISANAL COLLECTION SPRING-SUMMER 2017

Millefeuille, meaning 'a thousand folds', illustrates the multi-layering of several fabrics or garments within the same piece of clothing. Employed as *filtrage*, the technique can be used to imbue garments with illusionary textures or the traces of time.

MILLETRAGE

ORIGIN: ARTISANAL COLLECTION 2024

Milletrage – a portmanteau of mirage, *millefeuille* and *filtrage* – denotes featherlight garments posing as heavy-duty coats, jackets or trousers created from layers of fine lightweight fabrics finished with a visible fabric printed in the *trompe l'oeil* of a classic menswear textile such as tweed, herringbone or coarse wool. Finally, the garment is *aquarelled* with a voilette of transparent tulle printed to appear moon-faded, sun-bleached, tobacco-stained or oily as if illumed by the reflection of water at night. The practice reflects elements of the technique of *projective filtrage*.

MISFIT

ORIGIN: CO-ED COLLECTION SPRING-SUMMER 2024

Misfit is term applied to silhouettes spontaneously customised and resized with tape or work-in-progress stitching.

MONSTER

ORIGIN: ARTISANAL COLLECTION 2022

Monster is a term applied to any type of shoe which has been spliced together from three different vintage shoes dismembered and resized to create an *Artisanal* and/or *Recicla* piece, which can be industrially replicated as a *Co-Ed* piece. The technique originally appeared in the form of *monster* pumps and derbies collaged – or 'frankensteined' – from archive shoes created by fashion designers throughout the 20th century, including museum pieces and shoes from the personal collection of John Galliano.

NEO-ALCHEMY

ORIGIN: ARTISANAL COLLECTION 2021

Neo-alchemy is an overall term for techniques employed to bring out the authenticity in familiar wardrobe staples through scientific transmutations of shapes and textures. Realised in harmonious dialogues with the natural elements, these treatments uncover a lived-in look in garments and accessories associated with soul and reassurance.

NEW DÉCORTIQUÉ

ORIGIN: CO-ED COLLECTION SPRING-SUMMER 2019

New décortiqué is an evolution of the *décortiqué* technique in which the memory of one garment is cut illustratively into another garment, effectively altering its conventional values. It is the outline of a coat sliced into a cape, the silhouette of a safari jacket cut into a T-shirt, or the idea of a dance skirt evoked through incisions in a jacket.

NEW GLAMOUR

ORIGIN: ARTISANAL COLLECTION AUTUMN-WINTER 2017

New glamour draws on the idea of *unconscious glamour* in technical re-appropriations of items, which are traditionally and collectively experienced as seductive. Through this process, imagery and materials popularly viewed as simple or habitual are transformed through the familiar language of glamour. It is the illusion of rich organza made to look like rippled cardboard, the pattern of a skiing jumper knitted to resemble hieroglyphs, or fine lace formed through the tears of a dress.

NOMADIC CUTTING

ORIGIN: ARTISANAL COLLECTION AUTUMN-WINTER 2018

Nomadic cutting is a trans-mutative manner of cutting garments, which takes its name from the way it enables clothes to migrate around the body. Through deconstruction, pieces traditionally intended for the upper body are reconstructed into pieces made for the lower body, and vice versa: a trouser becomes a cape, a coat morphs into a short, a cape transforms into a halter-neck dress.

PLACAGE

ORIGIN: CO-ED COLLECTION SPRING-SUMMER 2022

Placage is the practice of fusing any two garments by deconstructing one and applying each piece to the other, effectively reconstructing the first garment in its original composition as surface decoration on the second garment.

THE POWER CUT

ORIGIN: ARTISANAL COLLECTION 2022

The power cut is a form of cutting whereby incisions made within a garment – typically through the method of *décortiqué* – evoke imagery collectively associated with ideas of power, such as a coat or jacket cut with *the memory of* the Geneva bands worn by judges.

POVERINA

ORIGIN: ARTISANAL COLLECTION SPRING-SUMMER 2020

Poverina or *poverino* looks are single garments spliced from several components such as a jumper, a shirt and a vest into one combined piece, their layers cut away to reveal the structure of the composition.

PRESSAGE

ORIGIN: CO-ED COLLECTION SPRING-SUMMER 2024

Pressage is a technique in which garments are laid flat and laminated across their natural drapes and creases to create unvarnished reliefs when folded out, effectively imbuing them with *the memory of* their own timeworn folds, or *the memory of* the creases that appear when garments are subjected to pressure inside a suitcase.

PRINTS WITH A PURPOSE

ORIGIN: ARTISANAL COLLECTION AUTUMN-WINTER 2019

Prints with a purpose is an overall term for the illusory or interactive properties of patterns and adornments, which embody the prints developed for the *Artisanal* and *Co-Ed* collections.

PROJECTIVE FILTRAGE

ORIGIN: ARTISANAL COLLECTION AUTUMN-WINTER 2019

Projective filtrage is an evolution of the *filtrage* technique wherein the impression of light projections on fabrics is adapted into actual prints on translucent materials. When overlaid on solid fabrics, these materials create the illusion of projected imagery.

RECICLA

ORIGIN: CO-ED COLLECTION AUTUMN-WINTER 2020

Recicla is Maison Margiela's term for lived-in garments and accessories repurposed through cutting to liberate the energy of age and reinvigorate the cloth. Designs carrying the white *Recicla* label – listing their provenance and period – are secondhand items handpicked by John Galliano, restored, and re-appropriated as limited-edition pieces, sold in the Maison's stores. A portmanteau composed from terminology denoting reusability, *Recicla* expands on the concept of *Replica* historically used by the house to brand reproductions of vintage finds within the collections.

REPLICA

ORIGIN: WOMEN'S COLLECTION AUTUMN-WINTER 1994

Replica is Maison Margiela's term for exact reproductions of historical garments and accessories. Designs carrying the white *Replica* label – listing their style, provenance and period – are replicated to precision from secondhand finds. *Replica* pieces are carefully selected as a representation of the shared history and recollections that underpin and inspire the communal values of the Maison.

RÉTRÉCIRAGE

ORIGIN: ARTISANAL COLLECTION 2024

Rétrécirage is a cutting-edge technique in which a tweed garment is strategically placed with elements of glue and fine wool crêpe which shrink the cloth when boiled and suppress the volume into a specific shape. Through this process, anatomical or coquettish sweetheart shapes can take form in tailored silhouettes, framed by an illustrative shoulder line.

RETROGRADING

ORIGIN: ARTISANAL COLLECTION 2024

Retrograding is a technique that embodies variations of thread-work, appliqué or encrustation – such as petals, godets, rosettes and ruching – which degrade from the bottom to the top of a garment. The practice illustrates the degeneration of detail that occurs when an image is imitated, or the linear base drawing of a painting that hasn't yet been finished. It takes its name from the astrological phenomenon of retrograde: the apparent lunar movement said to spin our energy inward and activate a deeper consciousness.

REVERSE DRESSING

ORIGIN: DÉFILÉ COLLECTION AUTUMN-WINTER 2018

Reverse dressing is the exchange of wardrobe elements conventionally worn as either top or bottom layers. Whether employed in styling or realised within the construction of a single garment, it inverts the traditional sense of dress: a trench coat may be worn casually under a dress, a jumper is thrown over a blazer, and a fisherman's knit manifests under a transparent skirt.

REVERSE SWATCHING

ORIGIN: ARTISANAL COLLECTION AUTUMN-WINTER 2018

Reverse swatching is a method which exchanges the fabrics traditionally used for certain parts of dressmaking with materials of a contrasting value. An active way of *appropriating the inappropriate*, eveningwear can be fashioned from bin-liners, foam or cotton wool, while sportswear is rendered in the fine fabrics of haute couture.

ROMPAGE

ORIGIN: CO-ED COLLECTION 2023

Rompage employs the ideas of *dressing in haste* and *appropriating the inappropriate* in the spontaneous customisation of dresses or other garments into rompers, mimicking the inadvertent gesture of getting one's dress caught in one's knickers. The technique also manifests in garments with hems cut in the V-shape of an unbuttoned body.

RORSCHACH CUTTING

ORIGIN: CO-ED COLLECTION 2023

Rorschach cutting employs *décortiqué* to create the subliminal subversion of one image into another through cut-outs within garments evoking motifs that trigger visual associations known to us all. Often founded in childhood memories, the imagery takes pareidolic form such as an American Western yoke cut like the ears of Mickey Mouse.

RORSCHACH DOTTING

ORIGIN: CO-ED COLLECTION SPRING-SUMMER 2024

Rorschach dotting is an adaptation of *Rorschach cutting* – patterns formed from cuts that evoke the outlines of familiar characters – into large thought-provoking dots created through cutting, appliqué, stencil coating and other surface decoration, which hints at iconographic and often pareidolic shapes known to us all.

SANDSTORMING

ORIGIN: ARTISANAL COLLECTION 2022

Sandstorming is a multi-disciplinary technique which, when applied to the surface of cloth or leather, conjures the impression that the article of clothing was subjected to a sandstorm. It is achieved through practices including fully engineered fabric weaves, needle-punch, flocking and beading.

SEAMLACE

ORIGIN: ARTISANAL COLLECTION 2024

Seamlace signifies garments constructed entirely from encrusted fragments of lace or other material decoupaged together, resulting in a completely seamless form like one big meandering embroidery. Created by hand, *seamlace* garments are some of the most painstaking and time-consuming ever created in the Artisanal atelier.

SHADOW PLAY

ORIGIN: ARTISANAL COLLECTION SPRING-SUMMER 2017

Shadow play refers to visual effects in which the illusion of a shadow is permanently evoked within a garment or accessory through techniques such as contrast swatching, flocking, or threading. The idea can also be activated by the layering of translucent materials and embroideries or cut-outs, actively casting shadows that become illusory embellishments.

THE SNATCHED

ORIGIN: ARTISANAL COLLECTION SPRING-SUMMER 2020

The Snatched is the *genderless* and multi-functional Maison Margiela bag continuously interpreted by the house in a variety of styles. Its name carries double meaning: With the bag's sharp folded edges, flap closure and clutchable handle, it hints at the British understanding of 'snatched': the swift grasp of an object, a gesture entrenched in the notion of *dressing in haste* key to the vocabulary of Maison Margiela. In contemporary lingo, looking 'snatched' is the ultimate accolade: an outfit impeccably put together.

STRIPE-TEASE

ORIGIN: ARTISANAL COLLECTION 2024

Stripe-tease is the practice of 'closing' the negative lines of a striped material – typically the blue-and-white striped cotton poplin of shirting – to create a colour-blocked entity, enabled by the sculpted – often corseted – form on which the garment is created.

THE TABI

ORIGIN: WOMEN'S COLLECTION SPRING-SUMMER 1989

The Tabi is the split-toed signature shoe of Maison Margiela, continuously interpreted by the house in a variety of styles and manifestations. Martin Margiela designed the *Tabi* in 1989 as a mark of respect of the *jika-tabi* worn by streetworkers in Japan. For the Maison's first-ever show, he transformed the traditionally flat shoe into a heeled boot and dipped the soles in red paint, allowing the boots to leave split-toed footprints as models walked the white runway.

UNCONSCIOUS GLAMOUR

ORIGIN: ARTISANAL COLLECTION SPRING-SUMMER 2017

Unconscious glamour describes the evocation of items or gestures that resonate as glamorous in the collective awareness. Founded in our shared memory of iconography across cultures and time, these codes imbue pieces or styling with seductive allure. It is the marks of white paint imprinted on a coat after one has unknowingly sat on a freshly-painted bench. It is the concrete imagery of a red lip, a décolletage, or a stocking seam; or, the implied effect of shrugging a coat off the shoulder, tying a pair of sleeves around the neck, or snapping a belt around the waist of a robe.

WET LOOK

ORIGIN: ARTISANAL COLLECTION AUTUMN-WINTER 2020

Wet look is a technique which permanently assimilates the impression of fabric soaked in water into garments, making them appear as if they are clinging to the skin. Employing *circular cutting* to materials such as butter muslin, tulle and *thermocollant*, the wet look effect is achieved through disruptive draping.

WORK-IN-PROGRESS

ORIGIN: ARTISANAL COLLECTION SPRING-SUMMER 2020

Work-in-progress is a manner of cutting, which freeze-frames the chapters of a dressmaker's process within a final garment. Here, 'unfinished' spaces yet to be stitched together are filled in with fabric inserts of a contrasting nature to the garment in question. It is the undone shoulder of a tailored jacket connected by a draped tulle panel, or the replacement of a blazer's lining with an organza underpinning bursting out from within.

JOHN GALLIANO

IN CONVERSATION WITH

PAOLO ROVERSI

Opposite: John Galliano, photographed by Paolo Roversi, Studio Luce, September 2024

FRANCES ARMSTRONG JONES: We are sitting here in Paolo's studio, Studio Luce, in the 14th arrondissement of Paris and I am wondering where and when you first met each other?
PAOLO ROVERSI: A long time ago!
JOHN GALLIANO: Long time ago, I know it was in London…
PAOLO: It was in London in your first atelier which was where, Portobello Road?
JOHN: It was Earl Street, by Liverpool Street station. You remembered recently my ping pong table, which was my office table then, so it must have been there.
PAOLO: Yes, you were in the middle of cutting material that you had just bought from Portobello, making patchworks and schoolboy/college uniforms.
JOHN: Being creative! *(laughs)*
PAOLO: You were already very creative. *(laughter)*
ALEXIS ROCHE: Who introduced the two of you?
JOHN: Well of course I knew Paolo's work as a kid, sorry student! Because it would appear in the pages of Italian *Vogue*. At Saint Martin's School of Art I would race to see it and the work in English *Vogue* with Lucinda Chambers, and Grace Coddington too of course. I mean if a piece of your clothing was in these stories that was quite major. Did you come with a stylist Paolo to meet me? Perhaps it could have been Manuela Pavesi or Anna Piaggi?
PAOLO: Yes, a stylist would have told me 'John Galliano is a young designer you must meet and see his work which is very interesting'. I don't know if by then you had already done a show, but I hadn't seen one before coming to your studio.
JOHN: It was really the early days, very soon after my graduation. The great thing is that those were the days when that happened, that curiosity. These guys would come to look at the work, putting the time in… it was amazing.
FRANCES: Do you think that doesn't happen today?
JOHN: Not in the same way, it happens differently, we all have access to everyone's work online. This was Liverpool Street station, the studio was very Dickensian, the steps were kind of crumbling, anytime you took a step another one would disappear!

FRANCES: Yes, it is very different, the time taken to go and meet someone and explore their world. Online is access but not the same.
JOHN: Yes, it's seeing the designer and his work in the place where it was born, the concept, the creation is always special. I think I was sharing that space with a photographer called Tom Mannion. We'd just left school so we were sharing a studio and when he had to shoot I would move to one end and when he wasn't working I could pull out the tables and the sewing machines and do my bit… it was open all night and it was great!
PAOLO: And you were working a lot?
JOHN: Yeah, night and day. You kind of move in and then you don't leave. Amanda [Harlech] who I was working with also, she would come down, with Lord Harlech too, and they'd sleep on the studio floor as well. It was a lovely beginning of my family, very special moment.
FRANCES: Paolo, do you remember the first pictures you took of John's work?
JOHN: It's just come up in my head like that… Chaplin, a young boy, it was Charlie Chaplin's grandson. Amanda did the picture with you and he was wearing pieces from the collection *Afghanistan Repudiates Western Ideals, Spring-Summer 1985*. It is really early days Paolo, so I hadn't done a show yet, this was from my first static show at Olympia. He was Charlie Chaplin's grandson, beautiful boy, curly hair and Amanda did the shoot. That would have been 1985. I just remember that image. I think that's my earliest recollection.
PAOLO: It must have been a Polaroid at that time.
FRANCES: So then leaping forward by a few decades bringing us to this story. Paolo could you please describe working with the torch and how these pictures are created and then John how you see your collection come to life through Paolo's torch?
PAOLO: You know working with the torch, I have written a book recently about light with Emmanuele Coccia. In it I wrote, 'Emmanuele once you told me that Plato was

thinking that we light our subject with the light of our eyes' and I think the light of my torch is the light of my eyes, the light of my heart that will go to light the things around me. *Voilà*, so the torch is really my light, that lets me light the world around me.

JOHN: I love the poetry in that. That torch seeps into you and finds your soul, because it's his eyes. I mean it's magical. The first time I saw Paolo work like that, I mean I'm not technical and there's a lot of science involved, and you hear shutter speeds and numbers and you wonder what's going on in that darkened room. Well, watching it is almost like a religious experience. Suddenly he's seeing the line [of the clothes]. Someone on set said, 'Why don't you try her twirling around in the dress?' and he says, 'No!' He sees the line, the textures start to appear, it's almost like a symphony or religious experience for me watching, a passage of rite or rite of passage... Painting with light, it's magical, it's just magical.

PAOLO: Yes, it's the light which is very mysterious and very sensual at the same time, like you touch the body and the textures with your light and every time is different, is unique. You can't do it twice the same picture, it is unrepeatable, and I love that. It is also very *éphémère* because you light and then it is finished – when you look it is darkness again. I like this too, it is a moment that passes, a vision. The light is there and then not there anymore and then there again. I like that.

JOHN: To be in that room in that moment is very, very special.

FRANCES: Creating these pictures for this story felt very intimate in the studio.

JOHN: That was what was so fab, the magic. We like teasing Paolo and giving him marks out of ten, but he got a ten out of ten very quickly with the photograph of Tish [Weinstock, Look 4] and we were like 'Oh wow where are we going from here?!' He '*mettre en valeur*', he just sees it and understands. Yes, it's definitely a one-off experience, it is the magic in the moment and the team around you and with you. It's just the moment.

FRANCES: It's very intimate in the studio because there are so many people in the room next door creating; the make-up, the hair, the dressing...

JOHN: The backstage if you like.

PAOLO: The maker room. I have never seen so many people as for this story!

JOHN: One thing I should add as well is that some of the muses had worked with Paolo, some hadn't and some were used to working in a very digital way. So to be allowed to enter the sacred space... We were briefing them before to be really still and not to move, the room will go dark but don't worry, we will all be there and then he's going to start painting you with a special light. Some of them were so nervous and some couldn't hold it still, a different generation, but in their faces you saw how grateful and thankful they were. They had been with a great master. Afterwards outside when the make-up started to come off and they were peeling it off [and able to speak again] they were waxing lyrical 'Oh my God it was such an experience!'

PAOLO: Gwendoline [Christie, Look 24] was very happy.

JOHN: Yes, she was so strict with herself, almost like a mime during the shoot and then after when she came back to see Paolo she said everything there was to say. It was beautiful, she's very articulate our Gwendoline. A really special experience for the younger muses who have never ever had that experience. Any slight movement and you let in a line that Paolo doesn't want.

FRANCES: Although sometimes a little movement can bring another level of magic to the picture?

JOHN: Yes, there was movement with Tess [McMillan, Look 3] in her hands.

PAOLO: I also love this one, she's like a broken doll, Emeline [Hoareau, Look 8].

FRANCES: John there were a few pieces that were made especially for this story that weren't in the show?

JOHN: Yes, we made some pieces. We thought we had to give Paolo something new that had never been shot before. For Monica [Bellucci, Look 45] the idea was to recreate the toiles in the process. To start with concept, the tarlatan, and then the toiles, but also go back a step from the finished thing as there's a rawness and it's still not completely worked out. We thought that would be really lovely for Paolo and we styled it slightly differently. Then I think I introduced some plastic as well.

PAOLO: I love the plastic.

JOHN: Yes, I thought that you would like it and the light refraction and Boldini's name being thrown out in the air. That's why I think I lost it when I saw Tish's picture. This is a BOLDINI!! So beautiful.

PAOLO: Yes, very Boldini [Giovanni Boldini, 1842-1931], and the Monica Bellucci piece is so beautiful with the plastic skirt.

JOHN: It was silk and we did a special finish on it that actually goes transparent with the finish. Monica Bellucci as a broken doll. The blouse was cut on the bias and then we did the similar treatment, those holes were individually cut which turns the whole thing into almost like a spider's web. Very lyrical, very nothingy, and it's on the bias so it's a beautiful way of working.

PAOLO: No for me it was a miracle to have to light this kind of clothes because sometime the clothes I have to light are so boring and flat. This was glorious to light. And the amazing shapes of the waists.

JOHN: Knowing and being a great fan of Paolo and admirer of him as an artist did kind of inspire us to go the next step. Even the gang were saying, 'Stop John this is like the beginning of a new collection!' Just the way that plastic reads like brush strokes, the white highlight on the plastic draped over foam is super interesting and I kind of knew that Paolo would capture that… the soul… *l'âme*!

PAOLO: *L'âme est la plus important.*

FRANCES: The models seem to understand so well the collection, the inspirations and how to hold themselves within the clothes. Do they work with you for a long time in the build-up to a show?

JOHN: Yes, I'm very lucky to work with them. I call them 'my muses' because they are so much a part of the creative process as well. They are family too, the Margiela gang. Seeing them in different guises as collections evolve is part of the story telling, part of the narrative that we own. Like I say, they bring so much emotion to it. There is a lot of emotion that spills from this work.

PAOLO: Yes, in the beginning I was thinking to bring more set and accessories to the story but in the end I decided to make just portraits, because as you say the muses are heavy with emotion and have such strong personalities. You don't need to put many things around them. My photography is more subtraction than addition. Not too much addition because I like to arrive to the essence of my subject. I like to look at my subject face to face. As John was saying, I like to see the soul of my subject, I don't want to be distracted by too many things. Here I have a beautiful person in beautiful clothes, that is completely enough.

JOHN: Yes, strong and brave. Peel away things that are not necessary but even the backgrounds are not *par hasard*… that metal or the treatment of the metal was giving so much as well. That comes with being brave, to take things away. The clothes were full of emotion, that was part of the inspiration too; trying to capture different emotional states, whether you were fleeing in the rain or trying to keep warm by wrapping your jackets in certain ways. The elements did inspire some of the embroidery and the finishing and that comes with working with the muses and the creativity they bring, which then inspired a way of cutting, so we called it 'emotional cutting.'

PAOLO: Perhaps we should change the titles from Looks to Emotions. Emotion number 20, Emotion number 24…

JOHN: With the coats, we said to Thomas [Riguelle, Look 24], 'Okay it's really cold, you've been by the river Seine, it's raining. You've had the best time of your life, you're walking home but you're not with your girlfriend, you didn't score that night'. Then I cut it to do that – it wasn't styled, those clothes weren't styled. You put them on and you get the gesture… emotional cutting. Which is a really fun way for me to work. With Mamuor [Majeng, Look 16] where he is holding the collar; the idea was that that was a guarded moment, 'don't want to be photographed', or something like that, but the coat was actually cut to do that. It was all spun off the body, one sleeve hanging… You know when you nonchalantly throw a coat on your shoulders, you don't look in the mirror, you just throw it on. Girls often do it, grab their boyfriend's coat and then it swings a bit forward. It was super inspiring for the cutting.

NATASHA MONTROSE: You have that in the tarlatan, don't you? The emotional cutting part?

JOHN: The tarlatan is kind of the concept, the beginning. These are severely tailored. There's more emotion in all the coats or the cardigans that were wrapped, you know the kind of old textile like this that had been rained on and knitwear but contrasted with a fully beaded skirt – the contrast, I love the contrast.

FRANCES: Turning to the photographs of the objects of inspirations for this collection, Brassaï [1899-1984] is there…

PAOLO: What John are in fact the inspirations for you? Is it what you like everyday or what is inside you already?

JOHN: Yes, it's so many things. You know there was a fascination with broken dolls or dolls that we've loved to death and that idea that you share everything with your doll, all your secrets, and then you discard her but imagine if she came back to you one day and she could explain to you, 'You see that life you've just had, I knew it was going to be like that.' The Brassaï pictures – I just love Paris at night, the wet, the rain, the refraction of light, drips, puddles, reflections of buildings in puddles… All those things that if you are 'OFF YOUR PHONE' you can enjoy!

PAOLO: Beautiful.

FRANCES: Paolo you have a photograph by Brassaï on your wall, what do you love about his work?

PAOLO: I love Brassaï. He is a real photographer, there are some photographers that are a little bit more journalist or literal. Brassaï is a real photographer. He just goes in the night with his camera, he is photographing Paris. I love all these pictures, they capture the soul of Paris. He is a great photographer because he was sensitive to his subject, at that time everybody was taking pictures of landscapes or famous people, not of people like Madame Bijou. No one was interested in Madame Bijou, but Brassaï was.

JOHN: When you look at all those characters, I want to know the narrative, where they are coming from, what they are about to do, how real they are in those pictures. I am sure some of them were perhaps set up, but it certainly seduces you. The lighting is very stylised and I am sure it wasn't *really* like that but my God it does inspire. If you look at those people, they weren't dressing up, that's how they looked, they walked the streets and existed.

FRANCES: Please can you explain John the title of this story, taken from a quote you said, that was also featured in the Artisanal film?

JOHN: *Would You Like To Take A Walk With Me Offline?* is something I said as an invitation to try and get people off their telephones. When you open this publication and see the photographs, it is offline, it's not digital. This goes right through the story, the passion, the time. It takes time to make beautiful things.

Opposite: Leon Dame, photographed by Paolo Roversi, Studio Luce, September 2024

Research book 'Brassaï', Maison Margiela 2023
Séville en Fête (1952) and *Fille de Joie*, *Quartier d'Italie* (1932), photographed by Brassaï
Opposite: Back of doll. Private Collection

Research book No.21 'Kees van Dongen', Maison Margiela 2023
Le Coquelicot (1919) painted by Kees van Dongen
Opposite: Porcelain doll. Private Collection

Research book No.19 '20's Beauty', Maison Margiela 2023
Portrait de la Marquise Casati (1911) and *Portrait de la Marquise Casati* (detail, 1923) painted by Kees van Dongen
Opposite: *La Môme Bijou, Bar de la Lune, Paris (1932)* and *Fille de Joie, Quartier d'Italie, Paris (1932)* photographed by Brassaï
Collection of Old Master drawings. All Private Collection

Research book 'Auntie Textures', Maison Margiela 2023
Opposite: Auntie. Private Collection
Following Spread: Leather bound process book, Look 2 and Look 4, Maison Margiela 2023-2024

Research book No.21 'Kees van Dongen', Maison Margiela 2023
La Femme au Grande Chapeau (1908) and *Portrait of Guus* (1906-07) painted by Kees van Dongen
Opposite: Antique doll. Private Collection

Research Book No.19 '20's Beauty', Maison Margiela 2023
Clara Bow (1928) and Louise Brooks (1923)
Opposite: Leather bound process book, Look 8, Maison Margiela 2023-2024

Research book 'Auntie Textures', Maison Margiela 2023
Opposite: Leather bound process book, Look 29, Maison Margiela 2023-2024

Research book No 21 'Kees van Dongen', Maison Margiela 2023
The Quai, Venice (detail, 1921) painted by Kees van Dongen
Opposite: Male Stockman torso. Private Collection

Research book '*Casque d'Or* photograph Les Apaches de Paris, c. 1900', Maison Margiela 2023
Research book No.19, '20's Beauty', Maison Margiela 2023
Madame X, lithograph by Kees van Dongen from the series *Femmes*, 1962

Research book No.28 'Irving Penn', Maison Margiela 2023
Portrait of Truman Capote (1948) and *Portrait of Igor Stravinsky* (1948) photographs by Irving Penn

Research book No. 34 'China Doll Masks', Maison Margiela 2023
Images of porcelain doll masks

'IT TAKES TIME TO MAKE
BEAUTIFUL THINGS.'

– JOHN GALLIANO

CREATIVE DIRECTOR
John Galliano

PHOTOGRAPHY
Paolo Roversi

ARTISTIC IMAGE DIRECTOR
Alexis Roche

STYLING
John Galliano
Alexis Roche

MAKE-UP
Dame Pat McGrath and Team Pat McGrath
for Pat McGrath Labs and Pat McGrath's team

HAIR
Eugene Souleiman at Streeters
Carlo Avena
Travis Balcke
Massimo Di Stefano
and Eugene Souleiman's team

MANICURE
Prescillia Demonceaux
and Gwenaëlle Navarro for Majeure Prod

CASTING
Jess Hallett

CAST
Yeray Allgayer
Monica Bellucci
Nyakier Buong
Valentine Charrasse
Gwendoline Christie
Rejoice Chuol
Sanija Dalecka
Leon Dame
Emeline Hoareau
Léa Julian
Chol Khan
Jum Kuochnin
Mamuor Majeng
Maggie Maurer
Tess McMillan
Natasha Poonawalla
Thomas Riguelle
Sherry Shi
Daimy van Betuw
Canlan Wang
Tish Weinstock
Hamin Yu

MONICA BELLUCCI'S
PHOTOGRAPH
Hair John Nollet
Make-Up Letizia Carnevale

PRODUCTION
Christophe Starkman, 109 Paris

And a very special thanks to
Maison Margiela
The loyal and dedicated Artisanal Atelier
The Artisanal team
OTB

PAOLO ROVERSI
PHOTOGRAPHY ASSISTANTS
Clara Belleville
Chiara Vittorini and
Marine Grandpierre

DIGITAL OPERATOR
Matteo Miani at Dtouch

VIDEOGRAPHER
Francesco Roversi

SET DESIGNER
Jean-Hugues de Chatillon

PRODUCTION
Studio Demi

Executive Producer Camila Mendez
Production Manager Caroline Daniaud
Production Coordinator Charlotte Moulin
Production Assistants Alexandre Gimenez,
Alexandre Costes and Layan Ghanem

POST-PRODUCTION
RetouchGradingBureau

LUNCHEON
Editor and Publisher Frances Armstrong Jones
Managing Editor Josefine Skomars
Art Directors Elena Feduchi, Giulia Garbin and Mariana Sameiro
Production Assistant Max Kallio
Marbling Artwork by Kyle Crooks
Printed by Graphius
Prepress by Dexter Premedia

Frances would like to thank
Tanja Ruhnke and Natasha Montrose
and Tiana Langdon at Maison Margiela
Silvia Sini and Jeanne Schmitt at We are the Agent
and Anna Hägglund at Studio Luce

PUBLISHED 2024

LUNCHEON EDITIONS

In this publication all photographs are copyright of Paolo Roversi.

Publication copyright Luncheon Magazine Ltd. All rights reserved. No part of this publication may be reproduced in whole or part without written permission from the publisher. Every reasonable effort has been made to trace copyright holders, but if any have been inadvertently overlooked, the necessary arrangements will be made at the first opportunity. The views expressed in this publication are those of the respective contributors and are not necessarily shared by *Luncheon*.

This *Luncheon* edition is printed on Munken Polar (by Arctic paper) which is FSC and EU Ecolabel certified.
Munken is an environmentally friendly and ecologically sound paper produced at Munkedals
in Sweden, which is one of the world's cleanest fine paper mills.
Graphius has used vegetable inks for this printing, partly powered by solar panels.